N
W E
S

SCANDINAVIA

Bergen

NORWAY

SWEDEN

NORTH SEA

SCOTLAND

Aarhus

DENMARK

(GERMANY)

Hamburg

IRELAND

Durham

York

Lincoln

ENGLAND

Cologne

HOLY

Oxford
Bristol
Bath   London
Salisbury

Ghent
FLANDERS

Speyer

ROMAN

Prague

BOHEMIA

St Omer
Crécy
Amiens

Rouen

Paris

EMPIRE

Neustadt

FRANCE

Champagne

A U S T R I A

Basle

ATLANTIC OCEAN

Poitiers

Limoges

SAVOY

Milan

Padua
Venice

River Rhône

Avignon   PROVENCE

Marseilles

Genoa

Florence

PAPAL STATES

PORTUGAL

(SPAIN)

ARAGON

CASTILE

GRANADA

Rome

Gaeta

(ITALY)

M E D I T E R R A N E

SICILY

Strait of Gibraltar

M   U   S   L   I   M   S   T   A

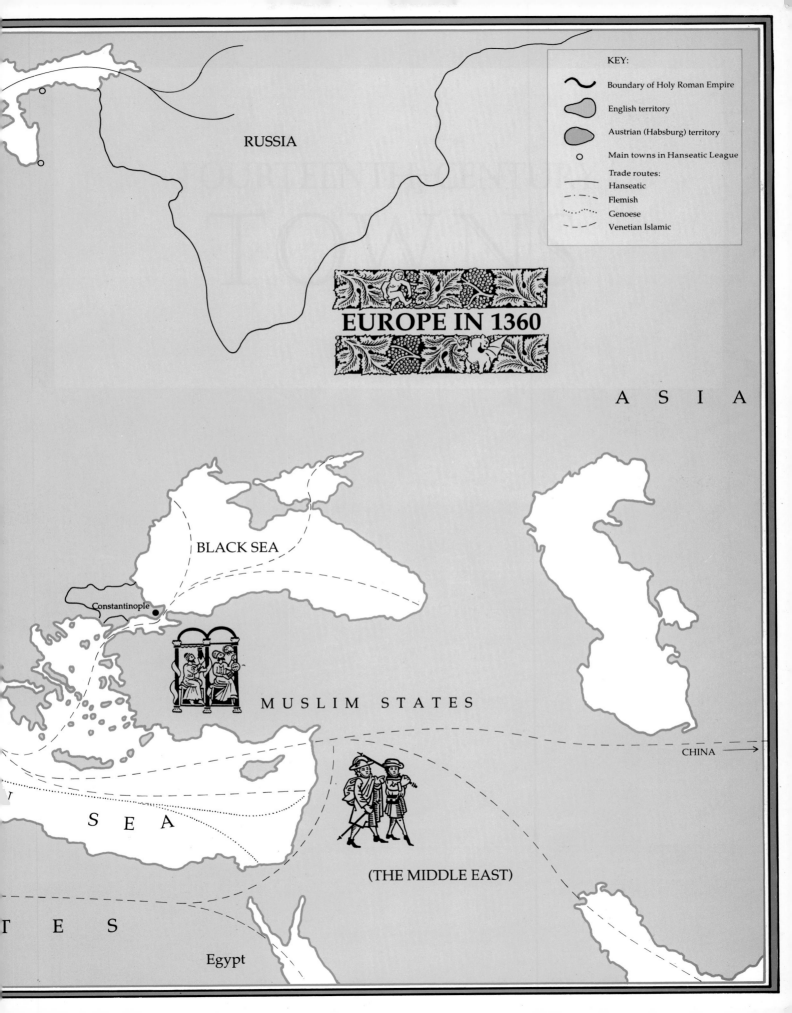

KEY:

~ Boundary of Holy Roman Empire

English territory

Austrian (Habsburg) territory

○ Main towns in Hanseatic League

Trade routes:
Hanseatic
Flemish
Genoese
Venetian Islamic

RUSSIA

ASIA

EUROPE IN 1360

BLACK SEA

Constantinople

MUSLIM STATES

CHINA →

SEA

(THE MIDDLE EAST)

Egypt

LIVING HISTORY

FOURTEENTH-CENTURY
TOWNS

JOHN D. CLARE, Editor

GULLIVER BOOKS
HARCOURT BRACE & COMPANY
SAN DIEGO   NEW YORK   LONDON

Requests for permission to make copies of any part of the work should be mailed to: Permissions Department, Harcourt Brace & Company, 6277 Sea Harbor Drive, Orlando, Florida 32887-6777.

First U. S. edition 1993

First published in Great Britain by The Bodley Head Children's Books, an imprint of Random House UK Ltd
Created by Roxby Paintbox Co. Ltd

Gulliver Books is a registered trademark of Harcourt Brace & Company.

Library of Congress Cataloging-in-Publication Data
Fourteenth-century towns/John D. Clare, editor.
p.   cm.— (Living history)
"Gulliver books."
Includes index.
Summary: Describes the institutions and daily life of towns in fourteenth-century western Europe, including home life, guilds, schools, the Church, and the ravages of the plague.
ISBN 0-15-200515-3
ISBN 0-15-201320-2 (pbk.)
1. Cities and towns, Medieval—Europe—Juvenile literature.
[1. Cities and towns, Medieval—Europe.   2. Civilization, Medieval.]
I. Clare, John D., 1952– .   II. Series: Living history (San Diego, Calif.)
HT115.F68   1993
307.76′094—dc20   92-13760

Directors of Photography   Bror Lawrence, Tymn Lyntell
Photography   Charles Best
Second Unit Photography   Bror Lawrence
Art Director   Dalia Hartman
Production Manager   Fiona Nicholson
Typesetting   Thompson Type, San Diego, California
Reproduction   Columbia Offset Ltd
                    Trademasters Ltd

Printed and bound in China

A B C D E
A B C D E (pbk.)

ACKNOWLEDGMENTS

Casting: Baba Rogers. **Costume designer:** Val Metheringham. **Makeup:** Pam Foster, Jane Jamieson, Emma Scott. **Props:** Eleanor Coleman, Cluny South. **Costume props:** Angi Woodcock. **Set design and building:** Tom Overton at UpSet. **Photographer's assistant:** Nicola Moyes. **Location manager:** Martin Gee. **Map and timeline:** John Laing. **Map and timeline illustrations:** David Wire.

Additional photographs: Scala, Florence p. 6; Reproduced by courtesy of the Trustees of The British Library (The Bridgeman Art Library) p. 6; Reproduced by courtesy of the Trustees of the Victoria and Albert Museum, London (The Bridgeman Art Library) p. 11; St. Andrew's Church (Lesley Coleman) p. 44; Archives Photographique Gerard et Adriana Zimmerman, Geneva p. 45; Kupferstichkabinett Staatliche Museem Preubischer Kulturbesitz, Berlin, photo Jorg P. Anders p. 55; Reproduced by courtesy of the Trustees of the British Museum (The Bridgeman Art Library) p. 62. Illustration by David Wire pp. 44–45.

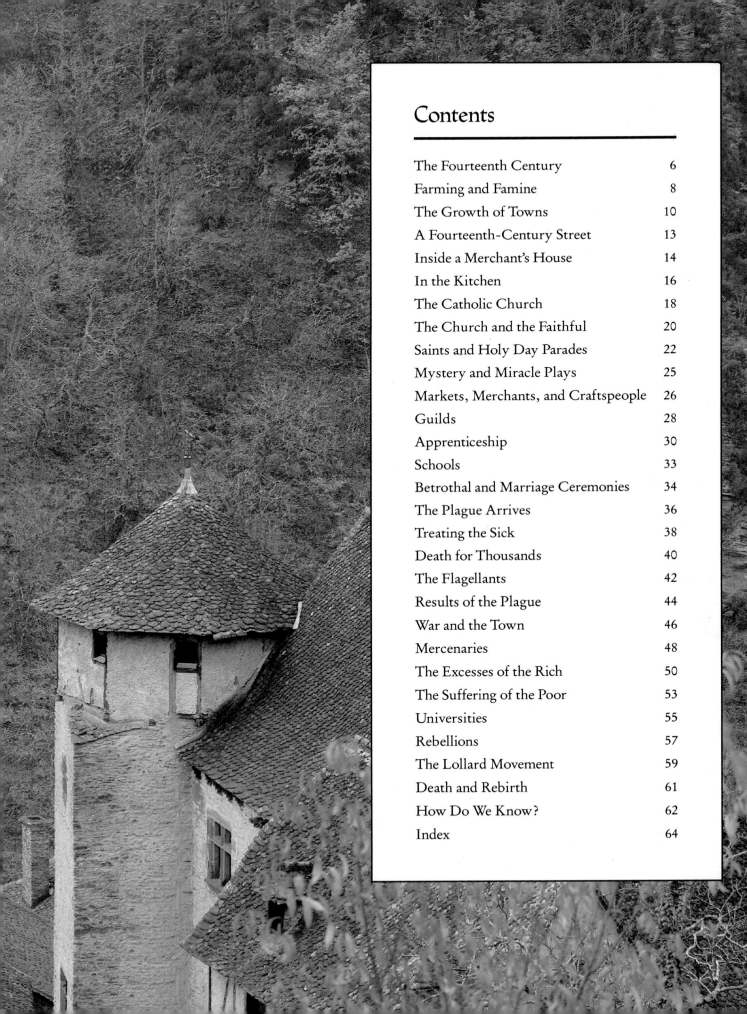

Contents

The Fourteenth Century

In Europe the 14th century was a time of knights, priests, and peasants, of war, disease, and celebration. It was part of a historical period called the Middle Ages, which lasted roughly from the fall of the Roman Empire in A.D. 476 through the Christian recapture of Constantinople in 1453.

A number of different barbarian tribes, including the Goths, the Vandals, and the Huns, dismantled the Roman Empire during the 5th century. For years medieval western Europe remained politically fragmented in thousands of small independent states. Although there was a king of France, his realm was divided into a number of counties and duchies, each with its own ruler. The Holy Roman Emperor presided over Germany, which was split up into more than 1,000 tiny states. Spain and Italy were similarly divided, with part of Spain under Muslim rule and one state in Italy ruled by the pope.

The Roman cities were destroyed or abandoned, but towns were at the center of medieval commerce and culture. By 1265 a group of northern German towns had formed a powerful trading association called the Hanseatic League. By 1300 many large towns such as Florence in Italy, Cologne in Germany, and Ghent in Flanders had gained control of the surrounding villages and had become states in their own right.

Outside the towns, medieval society in western Europe was based on what historians call the feudal system. At the top of society were kings and lords, who gave land to knights in return for military service. The knights rented tiny plots of land to

peasants in return for their labor. Many peasants were actually the knights' personal property; they had few rights and lived in appalling poverty and squalor.

Some women played important roles in government, the arts, and even battle during the Middle Ages, but generally men dominated government and society. A woman could inherit land only if there were no male heirs, and for most of her life she had to have a male guardian — a father, husband, or other relative. If she had no family, her feudal overlord could become her guardian. Women were not supposed to laugh in public and were taught to look straight ahead as they walked. One man in Paris told his wife to "copy the behavior of a dog, which loves to obey its master; even if the master whips it, the dog follows, wagging its tail."

THE NATURE OF LIFE

In medieval Europe, life was a struggle. There were few machines; everything had to be made by hand, and common items could be quite expensive — a pair of leather boots, for example, cost a plowman two months' wages.

For artisans and other workers, wages were low and unemployment was always just around the corner. Although the status of the poor and of women improved somewhat with the development of towns, they still had few political rights.

Poverty and violence were commonplace. Town records are full of stories such as that of William de Grymesby, a London shopkeeper: at midnight one Tuesday in January 1322, he beat to death Reginald de Freestone, an arrow maker whose singing and shouting had kept him awake.

Punishments, frequently performed in public, were often as brutal as the crimes. When Sir Gilbert Middleton was found guilty of robbing the bishop of Durham in 1317, he was dragged through the streets to the gallows, hanged, taken down alive, and beheaded. His head was sent to London, his body was quartered, and the four parts were sent to Newcastle, York, Bristol, and Devon, to be displayed as a warning to others. In many European countries an arrested person expected to be tortured; as the authorities questioned the accused about the crime, they might cut off a finger or toe, or stretch him or her out on a rack.

For the poor in particular, life was precarious. Two out of every ten children never reached their first birthday. Adults often died early because of disease, accidents, crime, or war. Little was known about hygiene or obstetrics, and women were in danger whenever they gave birth. Midwives helped the birth along, but if there were any complications both mother and child usually died. After giving birth, the mother was considered unclean. She could not bake bread, prepare food, or touch holy water until she went to be "churched" in a cleansing ceremony conducted by a priest.

IGNORANCE AND PREJUDICE

In contrast to European culture, Muslim culture and science were already highly developed in the Middle Ages. The Muslims controlled much of Spain, northern Africa, Arabia, and the Orient. Most Greek texts on mathematics, philosophy, and medicine were in Muslim hands in Constantinople, and it was Arab writers who introduced the concept of courtly love to European poets and troubadors.

But Europeans mistrusted people of other countries and religions. Hoping to gain control of the Holy Land, Europeans continually waged war against the Muslims, calling them "infidels" because they believed Jesus Christ was just a prophet — not the son of God — and because they considered another prophet, Mohammed, to be more important. In Europe itself, foreign merchants were frequently robbed, beaten, and murdered. In a story that shows both Muslim knowledge and European prejudice, a Muslim writer related how an Arab doctor dressed a wounded knight's leg and prescribed a refreshing diet to heal a woman suffering from tuberculosis. A European doctor, convinced the Arab could not cure the two, cut off the knight's leg, and removed the woman's brain and rubbed it with salt to drive out the devil, who he believed was causing her disease. Both patients, of course, died instantly.

Many European rulers and towns did welcome one group of "foreigners," the Jews, but only because Jews could lend money and charge interest on it — something that was good for a town's business but was forbidden for members of the Church. Many Jews became quite wealthy, but they were often forced to live in special neighborhoods apart from the Christian townspeople, and sometimes they were unjustly accused of drinking human blood, sacrificing Christian children, and performing black magic.

Far left: *A fresco of Florence painted in 1352.*
Above left: *A scene from the Luttrell Psalter.*

Farming and Famine

Only a tiny proportion of the medieval European population lived in towns. Most people lived in the country and worked on the land. Towns depended on the local peasant farmers to provide them with food.

Farming technology was simple. Oxen pulled plows, sowing was done by hand, and each year, part of the land was left fallow (uncultivated) to recover its fertility.

During the early Middle Ages the population grew steadily. Eventually these simple agricultural techniques could not produce enough food for all the people. When the weather became wetter and colder toward the end of the 13th century, things got worse. Crops failed. In some years during this "Little Ice Age" lack of sun meant that seawater could not be evap-

orated to produce salt, which was needed for preserving meat. Finally, between 1316 and 1325, large numbers of cattle and sheep died from murrain (pestilence).

Although people added wild rabbits, birds, and berries to their diet, Europe suffered more than 25 years of famine in the century after 1272. Many people starved. In some families, children were abandoned like Hansel and Gretel to feed themselves. One chronicler tells us that in 1315, hungry people ate dogs, cats, the dung of doves — even their own children — to stay alive.

Theft and robbery increased. Almsgiving (charity) decreased. Habitually underfed, the population was vulnerable to such diseases as typhoid, dysentery, influenza, and finally the Black Death.

This peasant family works from dawn to dusk in miserable conditions. The oxen are difficult to maneuver and the primitive plow cuts only a shallow furrow.

The Growth of Towns

Towns developed in the Middle Ages for a number of reasons. A trading center — a harbor, the confluence of two rivers, or a busy crossroads — often became the site of a market town. Other towns grew up around important monasteries or castles, where people hoped to be safe from attack.

Faced with hardship and oppression on the land, many peasants ran away to live in the towns. If they managed to avoid capture for a year, they became freemen. Once they had become longtime residents and had contributed to the town's civic life, they were officially citizens.

These growing towns were situated on land held by the local lord or the abbot of a monastery. The townspeople had to pay him feudal dues and work on his land just as the local villagers did. They hoped to receive a town charter from the king or a local nobleman; if they got one, the town became a borough and its leading citizens — the burghers, usually merchants — were released from the lord's control. Though they still paid yearly dues, or tithes, to him, the charter gave them the right to hold a market, to elect a mayor and a town council, to make their own laws, and to administer their own justice.

The strong wall around the edge of town helps to keep out bandits and hostile armies. Just inside the walls, around the edges of town, the poor live in hovels.

The marketplace, church, and administrative buildings are in the town center. Rich burghers live nearby. Their houses are built of stone in order to reduce the danger of fire.

Less wealthy merchants build timbered houses from wooden frames packed with mud, dung, and horsehair. Because land is expensive, they build upward. To provide as much space as possible, each floor juts out over the one below (this technique is called oversailing). Building plots are long and thin, and many have an alley down the side of the house for access to the warehouse and stables. **Right:** Many nobles keep town houses. When they visit town they pass through the strongly fortified gatehouse. There are few public facilities, so poor women do their washing in the river below.

A Fourteenth-Century Street

Fourteenth-century towns were surprisingly small. Few had more than 2,000 inhabitants. Even the largest towns, such as Florence and Paris, had populations of fewer than 200,000.

Nevertheless, hemmed in by their walls, towns were crowded and noisy places. Carts and horses clattered down narrow cobbled streets. Town criers shouted out news of fairs, marriages, and houses for sale. Beggars pleaded for alms. Peddlers and shopkeepers called out their wares — "Pepper and saffron!" "Ribs of beef and a pie!" Bells rang continually, announcing the opening of the town gates at dawn, the start of market trading, the start and the end of each working day, church services, council meetings, or the birth of a royal child.

Although town councils paid "scavengers" to clean away refuse, there were frequent complaints about the state of the streets. People threw their rubbish and excrement into the street or river. In 1365, Lincoln, in the north of England, smelled so bad that foreign merchants boycotted the town. People who could not afford to buy fresh water (brought in from outside the town by water sellers) had to take it from the public fountains, from backyard wells, or as a last resort, from the river.

At night thieves lurked in the dark, unlit streets. In some places the town council organized a rota of citizens who formed a "watch" (an amateur police force), but most towns simply closed the gates at dusk and rang a curfew bell. Law-abiding citizens closed their window shutters, barred their doors, and stayed inside.

A pieman and a water seller hawk their wares, a farmer takes his horse to market, a beggar asks for alms, and a few townsfolk stop to inspect the goods at a draper's workshop on this busy street.

Inside a Merchant's House

Often the ground floor of a merchant's house was rented as a workshop and a home to a craftsman and his family. On the second floor the merchant family had their main hall, where they ate and entertained. Other rooms, such as the solar (for activities like embroidery and reading), the parlor (for private conversations and business meetings), and the bedrooms, were located on the floor above. Very rich households had a small chapel and employed a chaplain. Servants slept wherever they could; often they had quarters in the attic.

Although houses did not have bathrooms or running water, people were concerned with cleanliness. Most towns had public bathhouses (Paris had 26 in 1292), and some people bathed twice a day. Numerous books on household management advised ladies on how to organize the cleaning of their homes.

This merchant family is quite comfortable in the solar. The wife cards wool with two brushes, disentangling the strands so that they can be spun on the spinning wheel beside her. Her daughter looks into the chest where the household valuables are kept. A carpet, too expensive to walk on, hangs on the wall.

Left: *Since the window openings have only wooden shutters, not glass panes, the merchant's chair has a high back and sides to protect him from drafts.*

Far left: *The merchant's children often play with a whip and top or with the bleached knucklebones of sheep. They toss the bones in the air, then try to scoop up another bone from the floor before catching the falling ones.*

15

In the Kitchen

Food was often scarce in the Middle Ages, and food costs were high. A peasant might work all day to be paid with three herrings and a loaf of bread. In one day, a skilled craftsman might earn around 4½ pence; a noble could spend 50 times that amount each day to feed a large household. During a famine, wheat could cost four or five times its usual price. In 1315 Lord Lancaster's household accounts came to 7,958 pounds for the year. He spent 3,751 pounds — nearly half the budget — on the buttery (a storeroom for food and wine) and kitchen.

A cook was a respected person and was well paid by the merchant or noble who employed him or her. Cooks baked bread, prepared meals, and set the tables. Only rich houses had cooks and ovens; most people had to take their bread dough to a baker, who would also bake their Sunday dinners.

Everyone wanted meat, but only wealthy people could afford to have it at every meal. Cooks served a vast range of meats, from beef, pork, and chicken to squirrel, porpoise, magpie, and peacock. They used herbs, spices, and strongly flavored sauces whenever possible — often hoping to disguise the taste of spoiled meat. An English recipe for "German broth" instructed the cook to boil diced rabbit with almond milk, cypress root, ginger, rice flour, sugar, and bugloss (a wildflower).

While the poor ate a lot of peas and beans, wealthy people liked few vegetables except onions. Some fresh fruits, such as apples and cherries, were available, but most fruit had to be dried. The rich drank wine; peasants liked ale. Only the poorest people drank water.

In many merchants' households in the towns, the kitchen is in a separate building; the oven and the fire — where meat is roasted on a spit — are a fire risk. The kitchen is a hub of activity — especially in wintertime.

The Catholic Church

Medieval life revolved around religion; everyone (except Jews) was required to belong to the Catholic Church from baptism until death, when he or she was buried in a church or a churchyard. Seven times a day church bells rang to mark times for prayer — though usually only monks and nuns prayed at every bell. St. Louis recommended going to mass every morning, but many people went only at Easter, when attendance was required.

People were especially concerned with what would happen after they died. Even if they managed to avoid hell, they expected to spend thousands of years in purgatory waiting to be cleansed of their sins. Only then would they have even a chance of going to heaven. When Pope Boniface VIII declared 1300 a jubilee year, in which indulgences reducing the time spent in purgatory were given free of charge, 2,000,000 pilgrims flocked to Rome.

In the Middle Ages a family often sent a daughter to a convent or a younger son to a monastery. Nuns and monks were supposed to live by the threefold rule of prayer, work, and study: they had to attend six church

services a day and spend the rest of their time working and reading the Bible. They vowed to live in poverty, to obey the abbot or abbess, and never to marry. In return, they were assured of a home and food.

During the 13th century, as towns grew more important, the orders of Franciscan and Dominican friars were founded. These monks lived among the townspeople, distributing alms, tending the sick, and preaching the gospel.

CHURCH AND STATE

The Catholic Church provided many essential civil and social services. Abbots and bishops acted as advisers to the rulers. The government and the nobility used clerics to write letters and keep records. Monks passed on knowledge, teaching and copying books by hand (the printing press had not yet been invented). In the monasteries, a monk called an infirmarer cared for local invalids, an almoner gave charity to the poor, and a hospitaler looked after travelers.

To pay for these services, kings and nobles gave land and money to the Church. In addition, the Church took a tithe (tenth) of the peasants' produce and of the merchants' profits. Some other ways in which the Church raised money — such as selling dispensations (the right to break a Church law, like the one forbidding Christians to trade with Muslims), indulgences, and benefices (positions in the Church) — seemed questionable but were also very profitable.

As a result the Church was both rich and influential. Pope John XXII was so wealthy that he paid 1,276 gold florins for 40 pieces of fine cloth. Bishops rode to war like princes, with large armies raised from their estates. Anyone suspected of disagreeing with the Church's teachings was called a heretic and could be burned at the stake. In 1302 Pope Boniface VIII issued the bull (papal law) *Unam Sanctum,* which stated that the pope had complete authority not only over the Church but over all kings and rulers. It declared that obedience to the pope's wishes was necessary for salvation — those who disobeyed would not go to heaven.

Many kings were displeased with the *Unam Sanctum*. When Boniface died, King Philip IV of France had the cardinals elect a French pope, Clement V, who remained in Avignon, a town in the south of France. Many clergymen wanted the pope back in Rome; in 1378 a schism (split) developed in the Church, and into the 15th century there were two popes — one in Rome and one in Avignon. Each one excommunicated (expelled from the Church) everybody who followed the other. This schism caused a great deal of pain; not knowing who the "true" pope was, no one could be sure of following God's chosen representative and getting into heaven.

Right: *Some friars, like this one, try to keep their vows of poverty. They distribute alms to the poor, while they themselves live by begging; townspeople often try to avoid them.*
Lower left: *When a young boy joins a monastery, he is given a monk's tonsure (haircut).*
Upper left: *Monks, who pay more attention to cleanliness than most people do, wash in the* lavatorium.

The Church and the Faithful

The cathedral's central position in the town, its size, and its expensive decoration reflected the wealth and power of the Church. Artisans who had little money themselves worked hard to beautify the

cathedral with carvings, paintings, and stained-glass windows. They believed this work was holy.

Yet people often found services difficult to get through. Many churches had no pews or music. The priest stood behind a wooden rood screen and led the worship in Latin, which few people understood. The artwork in the churches illustrated stories from the Bible, but many people still had questions about their religion.

Moreover, some of the Church's practices made people angry. In 1347 the residents of Gaeta, Italy, seized a papal tax collector, imprisoned him, and confiscated the taxes he was carrying. Reports about corruption in the Church were common. In 1340 an adviser to the pope investigated the monasteries and listed 42 complaints against the monks, including overeating, refusing to sleep in their clothes, having affairs with nuns, and plotting to murder the abbot.

A spirit of reform overtook some members of the Church. Groups of monks tried to imitate Christ; they disposed of their possessions and made themselves suffer by wearing hair shirts or whipping themselves.

But the Catholic leaders did not always react favorably. In the early 1300s, the Spiritual Franciscans were accused of heresy, thrown into dungeons, and tortured. Four of them were executed.

By the 14th century most of the great European cathedrals are nearing completion, having been started about 150 years earlier. The high walls (left) have been built by masons using simple tools, wooden scaffolding, and wheel-pulleys (below).
Right: *Inside, the cathedral is richly decorated. The services are long and are meant to be a mystery (wonder) to ordinary people.*
Bottom: *The Salisbury Cathedral clock mechanism. The Church is one of the first institutions to use clocks; the clergy needs to know when to begin services.*

Saints and Holy Day Parades

Medieval people believed they had personal relationships with the saints, who could offer them comfort or help. Most towns, guilds, and individuals had a patron saint. The Virgin Mary was considered particularly important. A saint might perform a miracle such as healing the sick, bringing the dead back to life, or making a statue cry. People often went on pilgrimages to places where miracles had occurred; they believed a pilgrimage was good for the soul and would please God and the saints.

Dozens of saints' days were celebrated as religious festivals, often marked by special plays, church services, and parades. The University of Paris observed 102 saints' days a year, and the city of Florence had over 120. On holy days (as on Sundays) the townspeople took a rest from work, and at certain festivals "the world was turned upside down": workmen ruled their masters, and pupils commanded their teachers.

For many people, a saint's day was not a time of worship but a time for fun. A town often held a market, and traveling merchants and peddlers mingled with the citizens, bringing the latest news from other towns. Although the Church criticized these activities, there was wrestling, dancing, ball games, cockfighting, and bearbaiting (dogs attacking a chained bear).

On the feast of St. James, a fragment of one of the saint's bones is paraded through the town in a silver reliquary while the people enjoy the holy day and watch the performers. Relics are considered holy; an object such as this one is a priceless treasure.

One church at St. Omer in France claims to possess a lock of the Virgin Mary's hair, a piece of Jesus' cradle, and a fragment of the stone on which the Ten Commandments were carved. People hope relics will be able to perform miracles.

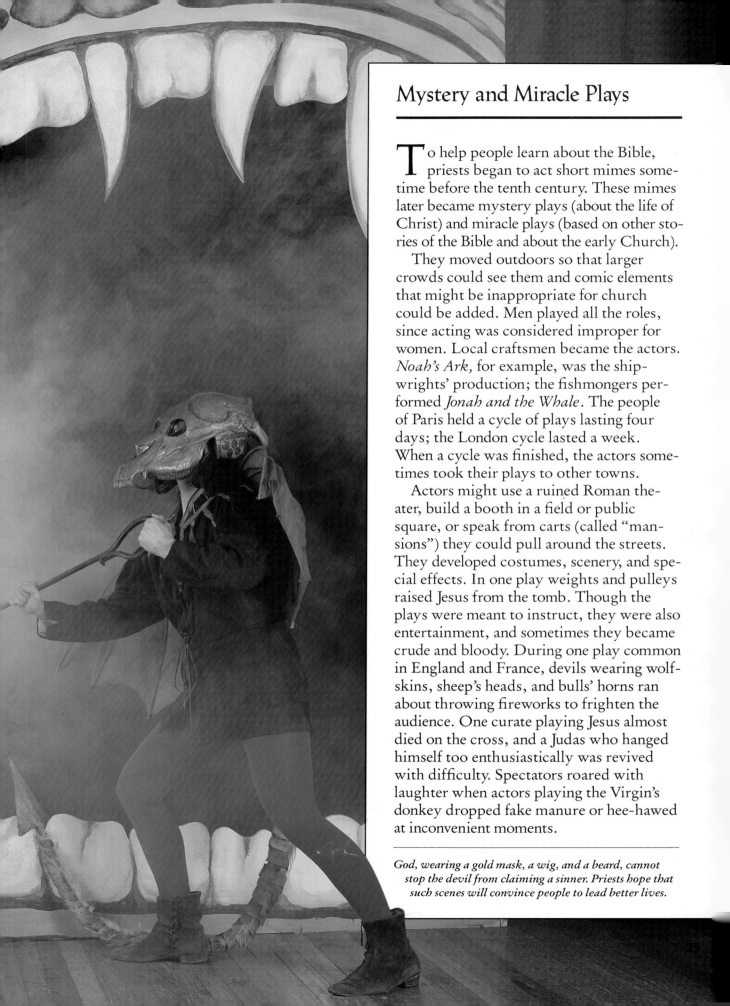

Mystery and Miracle Plays

To help people learn about the Bible, priests began to act short mimes sometime before the tenth century. These mimes later became mystery plays (about the life of Christ) and miracle plays (based on other stories of the Bible and about the early Church).

They moved outdoors so that larger crowds could see them and comic elements that might be inappropriate for church could be added. Men played all the roles, since acting was considered improper for women. Local craftsmen became the actors. *Noah's Ark,* for example, was the shipwrights' production; the fishmongers performed *Jonah and the Whale*. The people of Paris held a cycle of plays lasting four days; the London cycle lasted a week. When a cycle was finished, the actors sometimes took their plays to other towns.

Actors might use a ruined Roman theater, build a booth in a field or public square, or speak from carts (called "mansions") they could pull around the streets. They developed costumes, scenery, and special effects. In one play weights and pulleys raised Jesus from the tomb. Though the plays were meant to instruct, they were also entertainment, and sometimes they became crude and bloody. During one play common in England and France, devils wearing wolfskins, sheep's heads, and bulls' horns ran about throwing fireworks to frighten the audience. One curate playing Jesus almost died on the cross, and a Judas who hanged himself too enthusiastically was revived with difficulty. Spectators roared with laughter when actors playing the Virgin's donkey dropped fake manure or hee-hawed at inconvenient moments.

God, wearing a gold mask, a wig, and a beard, cannot stop the devil from claiming a sinner. Priests hope that such scenes will convince people to lead better lives.

Markets, Merchants, and Craftspeople

Two or three times a week most towns held markets, where local farmers sold grain, livestock, firewood, eggs, and milk. Craftsmen and traders from town erected stalls and sold bread, ale, candles, pottery, shoes, knives, and clothes. Most things were sold in bulk — grain by the bushel (36 liters), butter by the gallon (4½ liters), firewood by the hundredweight (50 kilograms). Cheeses were sold whole, whatever their size. Apart from barrels, there were few containers or wrappings, although but-

ter could be wrapped in the leaves of the butterbur plant.

In a typical town up to half the adult male population would be craftsmen. People of the same trade often lived near one another; modern street names such as Silver Street and Tanners Lane (tanners were leather workers) recall the occupations of the people who lived there in the Middle Ages. In York, in the north of England, all the butchers lived and worked in a street still called the Shambles (the name given to the butchers' tables).

These groups of craftsmen and tradesmen often organized themselves into associa-

tions called guilds. The guilds usually had strict rules about where, when, and for how long people could trade — it was an offense, for example, to trade before the bell announcing the market's opening had rung. Each town had regular assizes (meetings of officials who fixed weights, measures, and prices, especially of bread and ale). There were many other local rules; in London, for instance, fishmongers could only sell fish that was more than three days old — the fishermen had a chance to sell it first.

Most towns also had a market court, nicknamed the pie-powder court after the traders who sat in judgment there (the French phrase *pieds poudrés* means "dusty feet"). Punishment was usually made to fit the crime. Water stealers might have to walk through the town with leaking buckets on their heads, and a trader who sold bad wine would have to drink some of the wine in public; the rest was poured over his head.

TRADERS AND FAIRS

Merchants traded many goods throughout Europe and the Middle East. They formed partnerships by signing a *commenda* — an agreement whereby one man would put up money to finance a trip while another undertook the dangerous journey to foreign lands. They would then share the profits.

Instead of carrying large sums of money, traders used bills of exchange (a type of international check). Important banks grew up, especially in Italy, and Italian bankers became as unpopular as Jewish moneylenders.

The busiest and most financially rewarding trade of the Middle Ages was in cloth. Finely woven Flemish cloth was a luxury item, and the towns of northern Italy produced silk, velvet, and brocade, occasion-ally interwoven with threads of gold and silver. Italian merchants developed trade links across the whole of Europe.

Most international trade took place at great markets called fairs, held in large towns across Europe. Rich families sent their stewards to buy provisions for the winter and to obtain articles not available locally. Each town's fair coincided with a holy day, took place once or twice a year, and usually lasted two weeks. The fairs held in Champagne, a province of eastern France, were famous throughout Europe, and the king of France himself ensured that merchants could cross his country to reach them in safety. Still, as crossing France became more dangerous during its Hundred Years' War with England, the Flemish fairs in Bruges and Lille became most important.

Opposite page, above: *Few people can read, so shop signs show what goods or services are available.*
Opposite page, left: *English merchants sell coal, cloth, wheat, wool, and metalwork.*
Opposite page, right: *Italian merchants trade in luxury goods such as jewelry, glassware, embroidered brocade, silk, jeweled hats, and armor.*
Above left: *From the East come jewels, silk, carpets, and "spices" — everything from flavorings (such as pepper, ginger, cinnamon, cloves, and nutmeg) to medicinal plants and herbs.*
Above right: *The Hanse merchants trade in Scandinavian tar, timber, furs, rope, salt, goose feathers, and amber jewelry.*

Guilds

Only guild members were allowed to trade in towns. They could not work at night or charge less than a certain price determined by the guild. Members who failed to maintain high standards of workmanship were fined or expelled from the organization. By these methods the guild kept production down and prices up.

Some women were allowed to join guilds as butchers, ironmongers, shoemakers, hot-food sellers, bookbinders, and goldsmiths, but most guilds excluded women from full participation in social activities. A widow was usually permitted to practice her husband's trade. Domestic activities such as brewing, spinning, and silk making were exclusively female industries.

Many guilds provided a welfare system. The Guild of Mercers (dealers in cloth) in London charged dues each week and used the money to help poor members. Wealthy guilds started schools, ran retirement homes, and arranged entertainments on holy days. In some towns, leading merchants formed a merchants' guild. These guild members often took charge of town government when a charter was granted, and some even married into the nobility.

Wealthy people go to the tailor to buy fine clothes and hats. In the second half of the 14th century, laws try to ensure that people dress according to their status — with peasants often instructed to wear only black or brown. These laws, however, are impossible to enforce.
Below: *Buttons, introduced from the Middle East, are a novelty in the 14th century; most tight-fitting clothes are wrapped, laced, or sewn together on the body.*

Schools

In the 14th century, not all children went to school. A lord's son could be educated in a monastery school or as a page boy in a noble household, where he would learn mostly to hunt, ride, and fight. Wealthy

girls occasionally went to convent schools or had private tutors, and sometimes learned more about scholarly subjects than boys did. In France and Germany, some less wealthy boys and girls went to "little schools," where they learned religion, good behavior, singing, counting, and sometimes a little Latin. Sometimes monks set up an "outside" school, in a building situated outside the monastery walls, for local children who did not intend to become monks or priests. Young children were taught to read by the alphabet method, learning how to put the sounds of the letters together to make the word. Their first reading book was usually a psalter, a book of psalms of the Bible. But most children of the lower classes had no formal schooling.

As towns and trade grew, businessmen wanted a better education for their sons. Town councils, guilds, and some merchants set money aside to buy books and employ schoolmasters. The schools they established were called *Stadtschulen* ("state schools") in Germany, and grammar schools in England. They emphasized Latin — the language used for trade negotiations with foreign merchants — and arithmetic. The schools were for boys only. Most pupils were between the ages of 7 and 14. The pupils were taught all together in the same room. Work continued all day with only a lunchtime break, but there was no homework or private study as most pupils did not own any books. Lessons were often beaten into the boys. In Oxford, England, one teacher fell into the river and drowned while collecting branches to use for flogging.

Although grammar schools did not charge tuition fees, attending them was still costly. Pupils had to provide their own writing materials and textbooks, all of which were expensive. Nonetheless, the

boys still ruined them with greasy fingers, scribbled notes, and careless behavior.

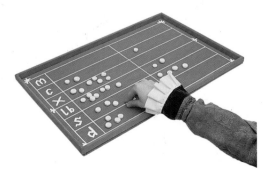

This grammar-school teacher reads from a textbook written in A.D. 350 by Donatus, a Roman teacher, then he asks questions.
Left, above: *A boy practices writing, using a stylus and a wax tablet. There are no dictionaries in the Middle Ages, so pupils invent their own spellings based on how words sound.*
Left, below: *Most pupils are taught to calculate using their fingers or counting boards. They also learn the religious significance of numbers. Three, for example, is the number of God (the Father, Son, and Holy Spirit).*
Above: *It is difficult to do sums using Roman numerals, so some schools have tally sticks.*

Betrothal and Marriage Ceremonies

For the wealthy, marriage was primarily the financial alliance of two families. Since a son came into his inheritance upon marriage, his parents often delayed the ceremony until he was over 30. Women usually married at about 20 but sometimes were betrothed (promised in marriage) when as young as 7.

Most wealthy people had little personal choice of a partner; marriage arrangements usually started with a business meeting to discuss the dowry and dower, land or riches the two families would exchange. Only then did the couple meet. Soon after, there was a meeting to read the contract, followed by the formal betrothal ceremony in the church porch. The couple exchanged vows

much as they would in the marriage ceremony, which also took place in the church porch. It was much like a modern wedding service — except that the bride always promised to "obey" and to be "bonere and buxom" (pleasant and easygoing). The groom gave the bride a ring, and the dower and dowry were bestowed.

Poor people usually married at the church gate, although a promise, or even a rush ring tied around the bride's finger, was sufficient to bind them. Witnesses threw grain and sawdust over the couple to wish them children and prosperity. All marriages, rich and poor, were celebrated with feasting and a riotous charivari (dance).

This girl's parents have arranged her betrothal to the son of a wealthy merchant. The agreement is drawn up by a lawyer; it is an agreement de future *(of the future), which is not binding. A contract* de praesenti *(of the present) constitutes an actual marriage and needs the pope's permission to be broken.*

The Plague Arrives

In the 1330s, stories reached Europe of great catastrophes in the Far East—floods, famines, locusts, and a plague that had killed two-thirds of the people. This deadly disease steadily worked its way westward along trade routes, reaching the Black Sea in 1345 and Egypt in 1347. That same year a Genoese fleet docked in Sicily "full of infected sailors, who died one after the other," as one writer described.

Giovanni Villani, the chronicler of Florence, described the disease: "There appeared certain swellings in the groin and under the armpit, the victims spat blood, and in three days they were dead." The swellings oozed blood and pus, and they were followed by spreading boils and black marks on the skin. Everything about the patient smelled foul. The disease came to be

called the Black Death, because of the color of the buboes (swellings).

No one was sure what caused the Black Death, though they knew it could be caught from other people. Citizens of the crowded towns suffered most. Guy de Chauliac, doctor to Pope Clement VI, declared you could catch the disease "just by looking at the sick people."

By 1348 the plague had spread to Spain, France, and England. The Scots, who in 1348 mocked the English for falling prey to the disease, died by the thousands in 1349. In the same year, an English wool ship, its crew all dead, drifted ashore at Bergen in Norway: the plague had reached Scandinavia.

Spreading along trade routes, the plague is brought into town by a traveling merchant who suddenly falls off his packhorse. A bystander discovers that he is already dead. Within a week hundreds of local people will be dead or dying.

37

Treating the Sick

The doctors "could give no help at all, especially as they were afraid to visit the sick," wrote Guy de Chauliac. "Even if they did, they earned no fees, for everyone who caught the plague died."

Many medieval doctors thought that all disease was the result of a poisonous miasma (bad smell). To overcome the miasma, a doctor would throw aromatic powders onto the fire or light tapers. To protect himself he might hold an orange or pomander over his nose. Some doctors made their patients sit in the sewers to drive the miasma out of their bodies. When the plague came to Avignon in the summer of 1348, de Chauliac sent Pope Clement away to a castle on the River Rhône, with orders to sit alone in a room between two enormous fires. It worked — Clement survived.

Only rich people could afford a doctor. When they became ill he gave them pills

and potions made from strange ingredients: cooked onions, ten-year-old treacle, herbs such as peppermint and aloe, metallic powders such as arsenic and sal ammoniac — even crushed emeralds.

But nothing worked against the Black Death once someone had caught it. Some doctors were seized by the plague while tending the sick and died before their patients. Others fled. "As for me," confided de Chauliac, "to avoid disgrace I did not dare leave, but still I was in continual fear."

A doctor examines the urine of a wealthy merchant who has recently fallen ill. He uses a urine chart to make a diagnosis from its color — the urine of a plague patient is blood red. If the doctor thinks his patient will die, he will break the flask, symbolizing death.

Another doctor holds a cloth soaked in vinegar over his nose while he treats the patient. Believing in the "use of opposites," he will counteract the fever by keeping the patient cold and making him lie still. In the meantime he lances (pierces) the boils, dresses them with an herbal salve (ointment), and removes any "bad" blood by bleeding the patient. It is important, he believes, to open only certain veins, selected according to the position of the stars.

Death for Thousands

In normal times, medieval people observed numerous religious rituals connected with death. A dying man, for example, confessed his sins to his family and a priest, made a will, and tried to correct any wrong he had done other people. As last rites, he had a priest pray over him and made a final vow of faith in God.

After a rich man's death his family organized a procession to carry his body, often draped in black, to the church. They held a burial service and laid him in a tomb inside the church. Men and women were paid to pray all night for his soul; in parts of Europe this "wake" was a wild party where guests wore masks, got drunk, and mocked the corpse. Poor people were buried in the churchyard, with or without a coffin.

During the Black Death, however, it was difficult to arrange a Christian funeral because almost all the priests had either died

or fled. In Venice uneducated boys sang prayers for the dead that they had learned by rote. In England the bishop of Bath and Wells declared that when no priests were available, anyone could give the last rites — even a woman, if a man was not present.

So many people died that it was almost impossible to bury them all. People simply dropped dead in the streets and fields. In Italy, wrote chronicler Agnolo di Tura, "none could be found to bury the dead for money or friendship. . . . Great pits were dug and piled deep with the multitude of dead." In many places, bodies lay rotting in the streets for days. Elsewhere bodies were buried so hastily that at night dogs dug them up and ate them. In Avignon, corpses were thrown into the river because the cemeteries were full.

In Florence the becchini — *local brigands, criminals, and poor men — board up the house of an infected family. For a fee they collect corpses and cart them to the cemeteries. The townspeople fear the* becchini *almost as much as the plague.*

The Flagellants

Medical historians disagree about which disease the Black Death was, but most think it was the bubonic plague and that it was carried by rats and fleas. Medieval writers were even more mystified. The bishop of Aarhus, in Denmark, blamed "the four stinks of stable, fields, streets, and dead flesh." Guy de Chauliac thought the cause was "a conjunction of Saturn, Jupiter, and Mars, which had taken place in 1345." Some people, blaming the south wind, built houses with windows only on the north sides.

Others agreed with King Magnus II of Sweden that "God for the sins of the world has struck the world with a great punishment." They sought to ease God's anger by living holier lives. Many people stopped swearing and gambling, and manufacturers turned dice into rosary beads. Huge religious processions were held.

Some men imitated Christ's martyrdom, hoping to obtain God's forgiveness. All over Europe, groups of flagellants, up to 300 strong, passed from town to town. They marched for 33½ days at a time (one for each of Christ's years on earth), scourging themselves and each other with leather whips tipped with iron spikes. Often the spectators cried, howled, and tore their own hair out. They tried to catch the flagellants' blood on their handkerchiefs, believing that it had the power to work miracles. But the processions actually spread infection.

The flagellants have promised to obey their leader and are not allowed to wash, shave, speak to women, or change their clothes. At each town they put on displays two or three times a day. If a priest joins the group, they must start all over again; they believe God no longer favors the Church.

The pope, fearing a revolution, will ban the movement in October 1349. Many flagellants will be arrested and put to death.

Results of the Plague

In all, perhaps a third of Europe's population died. The death rate seems to have been much higher in towns than elsewhere. In Venice 60 percent of the population was

lost to the mysterious disease. In Avignon 11,000 corpses were buried in six weeks. Medieval writers, overwhelmed by the shock of the plague, often exaggerated its effect. A French chronicler, for example, claimed that in Marseilles 50,000 people — more than the entire population of the town — had died. But some smaller places were completely devastated. When the Bishop of Durham called his tenants to-

gether in 1380, no one came from the village of West Bolden because they were all dead.

Eventually the Black Death left western Europe and moved on into Russia. In 1350 Pope Clement VI announced a jubilee year to celebrate the survival of humanity. A million pilgrims made their way to Rome to receive free indulgences.

The Black Death, however, was just beginning. Plague returned to Europe in somewhat smaller outbreaks in 1360, again in 1369, and then every 4 to 12 years until the 16th century.

REACTIONS

For survivors, the emotional pain of the plague was almost unbearable. "My sons Amerigo and Martino died on the same day, in my arms," wrote Lapo Mazzei, an Italian merchant. "And my daughter Antonia in bed, sick to death, and the middle boy with her. How my heart was broken."

People reacted in different ways. In Ireland, Brother John Clyn, the last surviving monk in his monastery, thought that the whole world was "in the grasp of the Evil One." He feared that all mankind would die. In Florence, the historian Giovanni Villani was more hopeful. "The plague lasted till _____," he wrote, leaving a space to continue the sentence — but he did not live to fill in the date.

In Austria "men walked about as if mad." In Florence the poor "became idle and unwilling to work." According to the Florentine poet Giovanni Boccaccio, "some people decided that wild living would keep them alive. They spent all their time drinking and reveling in tavern after tavern." Exaggerated fashions became popular; among the wealthy, both sexes wore tight jackets with slashed sleeves and large hoods, and "looked more like devils than ordinary people." Some of the poor took over the houses of rich families who had died, and behaved riotously. Anyone who developed a buboe was deserted immediately.

Many people reacted by looking for a scapegoat. They claimed that the plague had resulted from poisoning of the wells.

The Spanish blamed the Arabs, the French blamed the English, and across Europe people blamed the lepers. Anyone found with a suspicious powder was made to swallow it. Finally, in 1348 in Neustadt, Germany, a Jewish doctor was tortured until he "confessed" that a rabbi had given him powders to poison the wells. Led by the flagellants and supported by townspeople who were in debt to Jewish moneylenders, pogroms (organized killings) took place all over Europe, particularly in Germany. In Hamburg, Jews' houses were bricked up and the families inside were left to starve. In Speyer, Jews were forced to climb into wine casks, which were then nailed up and thrown into the river. In 1349, the citizens of Basle locked the Jews in a wooden building on an island in the river and burned them to death.

Below: *The Black Death causes deep despair among the people of western Europe, who become obsessed with death. A processional play called the* **Danse Macabre** *is common in many parts of Europe. These artists paint a fresco depicting the dance, in which Death leads the way and is followed by people from every level of society: the pope, kings, nobles, bishops, monks and nuns, minstrels, commoners, women, and children. An inscription will be added to warn the onlooker: This Is You.*
Far left: *A 14th-century stained-glass window in an English church shows death claiming a bishop.*
Above left: *the tomb of French nobleman François de Sarra, who died in 1360. Toads are eating his face and worms slide over his arms.*

War and the Town

I n the 14th century, war was considered an honorable occupation, although like the plague it caused many deaths. Many noblemen spent their whole lives traveling from one war to the next. Noblewomen rarely traveled to battle, but they did help with or even take charge of defending their own castles.

From 1337 to 1453, France and England fought what is known as the Hundred Years' War. After the battles of Crécy (1346) and Poitiers (1356) — both disastrous for the French cavalry — military commanders tried to avoid pitched battles. Instead, the two armies raided the French countryside, burning crops in an attempt to starve the enemy. These destructive raids, called *chevauchées,* caused famine and hardship for the French peasants.

Sometimes an army would besiege a town, camping outside the walls and pre-

venting food and other supplies from reaching the citizens. The local militia would defend the walls, firing arrows, throwing large stones, and making surprise attacks on the besiegers. But they could do little to save the town. In the end townspeople were often reduced to eating dogs, cats, and even rats and excrement. The siege ended when the starving townspeople surrendered, or when the army tunneled under the walls and invaded the town.

After a long siege, a bored and frustrated army often massacred a town's entire population. When Limoges was captured in 1370, only the bishop of Limoges and the three French knights who had led the defense were spared. The 3,000 other citizens begged for mercy, but the English soldiers slit their throats.

In 1373, during a British chevauchée lasting six months, the French army follows close on the heels of the invaders. The English are destroying the countryside and slaughtering peasants, but the French refuse to risk starting a real battle.

Mercenaries

During the lulls between the campaigns of the Hundred Years' War, the French and English armies were dissolved and large bands of unemployed soldiers were left wandering the countryside. These groups, called Free Companies, were made up of mercenaries, men prepared to fight for any government or city that would pay them.

Left on their own, they often attacked and plundered towns. Bascot de Mauleon claimed that he had made a fortune from "robbery, protection money, and strokes of luck." The French knight Bertrand de Guesclin admitted that he had "attacked women, burned houses, killed children, and taken men ransom." The people of one village threw themselves into the river when they heard that Sir Robert Knollys was coming. "When we rode out, the country

trembled before us," boasted one knight.

Sometimes mercenaries could be bribed to go away. When a company led by de Guesclin passed through Avignon it received 200,000 francs and a blessing from the pope, who remarked ruefully that people normally paid him, not robbed him, to be blessed.

Many of the knights and nobles who led Free Companies were rewarded by their governments and accepted into wealthy society. After years of killing, Eustace d'Aubrecicourt married a niece of the queen of England. Some people did complain, however; the French writer Jean de Vinette criticized the knights and blamed the government for not defending his country against the marauders.

The Church teaches that knights protect the people. These wealthy townspeople, whose possessions are being stolen, know that this is not true.

The Excesses of the Rich

In the Middle Ages people loved feasting and the "delight of meats." This was especially true after the Black Death, when the rich people in town and countryside decided to enjoy life while they could and "abandoned themselves to the sin of gluttony."

Their feasts were extravagant displays of wealth and plenty — cooks sometimes gilded meats with real gold dust. In 1368, citizens of Milan were amazed when their duke gave his daughter Violante Visconti a wedding feast comprised of 30 courses of meat and fish, including suckling pig with crabs, hare with pike, and calf with trout. The leftover food alone fed a thousand servants and beggars. In between each course the host presented gifts of armor, falcons,

horses, war dogs, and fat oxen to the groom's men.

Hosts tried to surprise their guests with sensational gimmicks. Often they trapped small live birds in a pie shell; the birds flew out when the crust was cut, then servants released hawks to hunt them. Peacocks and swans were roasted, then served with their feathers carefully replaced. At a feast in Savoy guests were served by mounted knights who carried the food on plates attached to the points of their lances. At a banquet in France the ceiling opened and the food was lowered on machines disguised to look like clouds. The final course was accompanied by a shower of scented water and sweet-meats (candied fruits).

Sitting on benches, guests eat with knives, spoons, and fingers — forks are rare. Guests use their little fingers to take rich sauces from the bowls on the table. Few families own plates, so food is served on thick slices of bread, which will later be distributed to the poor.

The Suffering of the Poor

The Black Death, combined with the destruction caused by the Hundred Years' War and the bad weather, seriously damaged western Europe's economy. Many towns declined, particularly in Italy. Trade had almost ceased during the plague; now, with so many lawyers dead, it was delayed by a backlog of lawsuits and requests for new contracts. There were not enough laborers to cultivate the land, so food was in short supply and prices went so high that workers' wages could not keep up. Desperate people were driven to steal, and the crime rate increased. Meanwhile, the population continued to fall.

Old people, who had to rely on others to look after them, suffered most. The elderly usually handed over ownership of their business and home to a son or neighbor, then moved into a room in the house so the family could look after them. But once burdened with the "labor of washing and the cost of heating," the son and daughter-in-law often were tempted to neglect their aging relatives. Inquests revealed that many old people were left to look after themselves. One old lady fell into a well while trying to fetch water; another drowned in a stream when she left her son's house to beg for bread in a nearby town.

This old man's children died in the plague. Now alone in his one-room hut, he lives on a diet of vegetable stew,

pease pudding (boiled dried peas), and bean-flour bread. Like many peasants, he keeps a pig; it shares his cottage and his food.
Above top: *A moderately well-off peasant returns home to a flint house with a load of kindling.*
Above: *The walls of many peasants' huts are made of wattle and daub. Not as strong as flint, the interwoven sticks smeared with clay at least keep out the worst of the weather.*

Universities

So many learned men died from the Black Death that a number of universities and colleges were founded to train new scholars.

The most famous were the University of Prague (1348) and New College, Oxford (1379). Teachers aimed to spread traditional thinking, not to develop new ideas; any lecturer who spoke against the Church's teachings had to admit his error publicly and promise to "hold to the Catholic faith."

Conditions were harsh. New students in France and Scotland had to suffer the *bejan* (initiation ceremony), in which older students bullied and washed them in public. No university let students have fires in their rooms — yet windows lacked glass panes and usually were covered only by drafty wooden shutters.

Although scholars (and their teachers) were mostly clerics preparing for careers in the Church, they were sometimes violent. University rules forbade students to knife an examiner who asked a difficult question — which gives some idea of how students behaved. Often there was undeclared war between town and gown (townspeople and students); students were poor and undisciplined, but townspeople needed their business to make a living. In 1355 a mob of local people invaded Oxford University and assaulted, killed, or scalped a number of students.

Undergraduates, who are usually between 12 and 18 years old, live and are taught in groups of about a dozen in halls (houses rented to teachers). They study the **trivium** *(grammar, rhetoric, and logic) and the* **quadrivium** *(arithmetic, geometry, astronomy, and music), and may specialize in medicine or law. A degree course lasts six years. Colleges (main picture) are only for postgraduates.*
Left: Precious, handwritten books are often kept safely chained in a chest.
Below: Many lecturers merely read from a book. Some students follow the text in their own books, while others chatter or sleep.

Rebellions

During the plague, craftsmen and laborers realized that the shortage of workers increased their bargaining power. For example, in June 1349, when the Black Death raged in the French town of Amiens, the tanners there demanded higher wages. Prices rose, and the wealthy found they needed more money to maintain their standard of living. To reduce prices, governments passed laws forbidding workers to take higher wages, or to buy fine clothes and food with those wages.

Writers noted that the laborers were "filled with a spirit of rebellion." In 1358, French peasants organized a rebellion called the Jacquerie (after the padded jackets the peasants wore in battle). They burned some castles and killed a few nobles. Jean Froissart, who disapproved of the rebellion, probably exaggerated the harm done when he recorded that there were 100,000 rebels and that "never did men commit such vile deeds: I could never bring myself to write down what they did to the ladies."

In 1381 the weavers of Ghent rebelled against the Count of Flanders. In England 20,000 peasants, led by an old soldier named Wat Tyler, marched on London to demand that "lords be no more masters than ourselves." In Paris and Rouen the Maillotins (named after the 3,000 police mallets they seized) murdered many Jews and wealthy people.

Eventually, however, all the rebellions were put down — the peasants were no match for mounted knights. "The nobles," wrote Froissart, "wiped them out wherever they found them, without mercy or pity."

Crying, "Viva il popolo!" ("Long live the people!"), the Florentine ciompi (workers of the lowest class) seize power in 1378. They demand the right to join guilds and the freedom to form trade unions. Their government will last only 41 days.

58

The Lollard Movement

After the Black Death, many people felt the Church had let them down. Although half the clergy had died, people accused priests of deserting their flocks and fleeing from the plague. They said that priests were only interested in wealthier parishes and higher wages.

In the 1370s John Wyclif, a teacher at Oxford, claimed that the Church was too wealthy and urged people to stop paying tithes. Wyclif had the Bible translated from Latin into English, allowing ordinary people to understand it for the first time. He argued that priests were not necessary for salvation, and denied transubstantiation, an important Church teaching that says that during a mass bread and wine turn into the actual body and blood of Christ.

Wyclif's influence spread across Europe as his followers, called Lollards, went into the countryside preaching and reading people the Bible in their native languages. Many Lollards were more extreme than Wyclif himself; Sybil Godsell said that women ought to be allowed to become priests, and another woman, Hawise Moone, wanted to give the wealth of the Church to the poor. Some Lollards claimed that war was evil and refused to fight in the army.

Church authorities accused the Lollards of being heretics. In the early 1400s a number of Wyclif's supporters were burned at the stake. Though the movement appeared to die out, some Lollards continued to meet in secret. A century later, during the period of religious changes called the Reformation, many people in northern Europe accepted similar ideas.

John Badby, a Lollard, has refused to accept the doctrine of transubstantiation. He has been taken to Smithfield, outside London, and is about to be burned to death.

Death and Rebirth

The modern historian Barbara Tuchman has described the 14th century as "a succession of wayward dangers" — a time when humanity seemed at the mercy of famine, animal murrain, the Black Death, war, mercenaries, rebellion, and heresy. According to a 14th-century Italian chronicler, "People said and believed, 'This is the end of the world.'"

But with the dangers came unexpected and sometimes exciting changes. Money lavished on building cathedrals and colleges led to developments in architecture, painting, and sculpture. Nobles who spent extravagantly on feasting and fashionable clothes enriched the tradesmen. Even war sometimes had its advantages — the Italian merchant Rinaldo degli Albizzi wrote that in time of war "the city is always full of soldiers, who must buy all their needs; tradesmen grow prosperous." Medical knowledge increased after the Black Death as doctors began to write manuals based on their professional experiences rather than simply accepting the opinions of ancient Greek writers. The Lollards and the peasant revolts of the 14th century were the first signs of Protestantism and democracy (government by the people).

After the delay caused by the plague, international commerce also continued to develop. Books brought from the Muslim East expanded western Europe's knowledge, especially of mathematics and geography, and Europeans began to seek new trade routes and markets. Eventually this led to Columbus's voyage to the Americas in 1492.

The world did not end in the 14th century, as some people had predicted it would. With the 15th and 16th centuries came further developments in art, politics, and religion. These years, later known as the Renaissance ("rebirth") and the Reformation, ushered in a new era in Europe.

Despite the wars, plagues, and famines of the 14th century, life goes on. Here nobles, traders, peasants, and beggars wait for the town gates to open. This medieval town is small, but it is a vitally important center of trade, government, religion, learning, and new ideas.

How Do We Know?

In the 14th century ordinary people began to keep records. Many of their documents have survived, such as records of court cases, rent books, recipes, letters, and guild regulations. People also began to write in their own languages instead of in Latin; from the 14th century, for instance, comes the earliest example of a letter written by a woman in English. Many government documents and clerics' writings also survive.

Documents dating from the Middle Ages are difficult to read. In some cases the ink has faded completely. Where it is still visible, it is often illegible. Medieval handwriting was often a badly formed scrawl, and people spelled words however they liked. Historians are not the only people who have had problems as a result. Doing his household accounts in 1315, Lord Lancaster had to write off 242 pounds "for things bought, whereof cannot be read in my note."

It was also common practice to rub out the writing on an old document and reuse the parchment. A manuscript on which two or more texts have been written is called a palimpsest. The poet Giovanni Boccaccio, visiting the famous library at Monte Cassino in Italy before the Black Death arrived, found the monks erasing priceless manuscripts so that they could copy out reading books to sell to the local schoolchildren.

Nevertheless, some beautiful books have survived from the 14th century. The Luttrell Psalter is full of detailed drawings of country people. The *Très Riches Heures,* a book of prayers commissioned by the duke of Berry, contains scenes of country life. Monks who illuminated the Bible illustrated the stories as if the action had taken place in medieval times; the characters are in medieval clothes, set against medieval backgrounds. These pictures are valuable for historians, who can use them to see how people lived in the Middle Ages.

FACT AND FICTION

Many chronicles (histories) have survived from the 14th century. The best is perhaps Jean Froissart's account of the Hundred Years' War between France and England. Froissart gathered his information himself — for instance, he interviewed the Free Company leader Bascot de Mauleon. His witnesses almost certainly exaggerated their stories, though, and then Froissart tried to make the people he wrote about seem even more glamorous; he admitted that he wrote "so that men should be inspired to follow such examples." Froissart, a Frenchman, was biased in favor of the French, and he never criticized "the most noble Count of Blois," who was his employer.

Medieval writing often followed a formula. When describing disasters or corruption, writers automatically echoed the ideas and language of the Bible. In *The Flowers of History,* for example, Matthew of Westminster described the Scottish leader William Wallace as "more hardened in cruelty than Herod." Matthew could have been referring to any soldier in any army — the description is a standard one, even down to the details of what Wallace did, such as burning children to death and setting fire to churches. Because a chronicle might include such stories only as standard formulas for military atrocities, the historian has to decide whether or not they are true.

In addition to chronicles, historians can turn to poems and stories written in the 14th century, such as John Langland's *Piers Plowman*, Boccaccio's *Decameron,* and Geoffrey Chaucer's *Canterbury Tales*. In *Piers Plowman,* Langland described the life of a peasant and suggested ways both laymen and members of the Church could improve their lives; his work was more widely known to 14th-century Britons than any other, except some ballads and mystery plays. Both Boccaccio and Chaucer included realistic descriptions of typical characters — useful to a historian who wishes to know how people behaved in everyday life. In addition, Boccaccio and Chaucer described what these people were thinking. The rude stories in the *Decameron* show the despair and worldliness of the years just after the plague. In Chaucer's tales we see a full range of human characteristics and attitudes — from respect for Christians of true faith to mistrust of dishonest clergymen, and from chivalry to moderate feminism and crude humor.

LEGENDS AND ISSUES

Using these sources, the historian tries to work out what life was really like. This task can be difficult. For instance, how clean did medieval people keep themselves? Contemporary writers complained of the peasants' foul smell and of the "beer, grease, bones, and excrement" mixed in the straw on house floors. Basing their arguments on such sources, many historians have said that medieval families lived in total squalor. Yet we know that towns had bathhouses and that wealthy people tried to make rooms smell pleasant.

What is the historian to believe? Do the frequent complaints about debris in the streets show that medieval people lived in filthy conditions? Or do they show that people objected to the rubbish and were taking steps to make their towns clean?

A NOTE ABOUT MONEY

Estimating what money was worth in the Middle Ages is difficult because the relative prices of goods were so different from what they are now. For example, in the Middle Ages 240 sheets of parchment cost 10 shillings — almost as much as a cow. All prices need to be considered in relation to the incomes of the people of the time: a British laborer's daily wage was around 4 pence, and a knight's daily wage in battle was 2 shillings (or 24 pence), while the income of a rich lord might be 8,000 pounds a year (or 1,920,000 pence). An English pound was worth an actual pound of silver, but the most widely accepted coin in Europe was the gold florin of Florence.

WORDS FROM THE PAST

Dom Ramon Muntaner, a Spanish soldier, left home when he was 10; over the years he traveled far and fought in 32 battles. In 1325, when he was 60, he sat down to write his memoirs. He wrote, "I would gladly avoid the task of this story; yet it is my bounden duty to tell it, so that everybody will learn how the grace of God is the best help in danger." It is exciting to think that you are reading the exact words and thoughts of someone who lived more than 600 years ago. Did Dom Ramon, perhaps, pause to wonder if anyone would be reading his words or hearing about his world hundreds of years later? If he did, he was thinking of *you*. Across the centuries, your minds can meet: you are thinking of him, and he is speaking to you.

Above left: *A picture from the Luttrell Psalter shows Sir Geoffrey Luttrell with his wife and daughter-in-law.*

● Italian explorer Marco Polo visits China (1271)

THE HUNDRED YEARS W

Fall of Acre:
end of the Crusades
(1291) ●

Philip IV, King of France (1285 – 1314) ●————————————●

Froissart, French chronicle

Pope Boniface VIII (1294 – 1303) ●———●

Italian p

Petrarch, Italian poet laureate (1304 – 1374) ●————————————

Chaucer, English wri

1280	1290	1300	1310	1320	1330	1340

The end of ten years of
devastating animal murrain

Great Famine in Europe

The
The

Battle

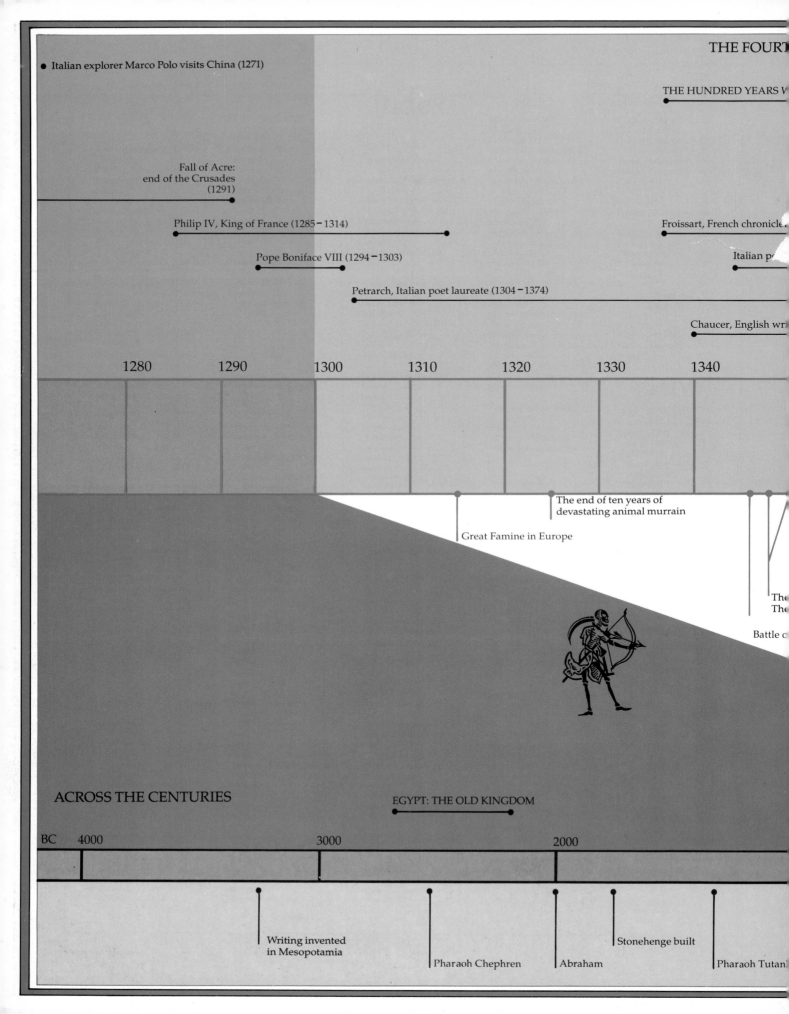

ACROSS THE CENTURIES

EGYPT: THE OLD KINGDOM ●————————————●

BC	4000	3000	2000

Writing invented
in Mesopotamia

Pharaoh Chephren

Abraham

Stonehenge built

Pharaoh Tutan

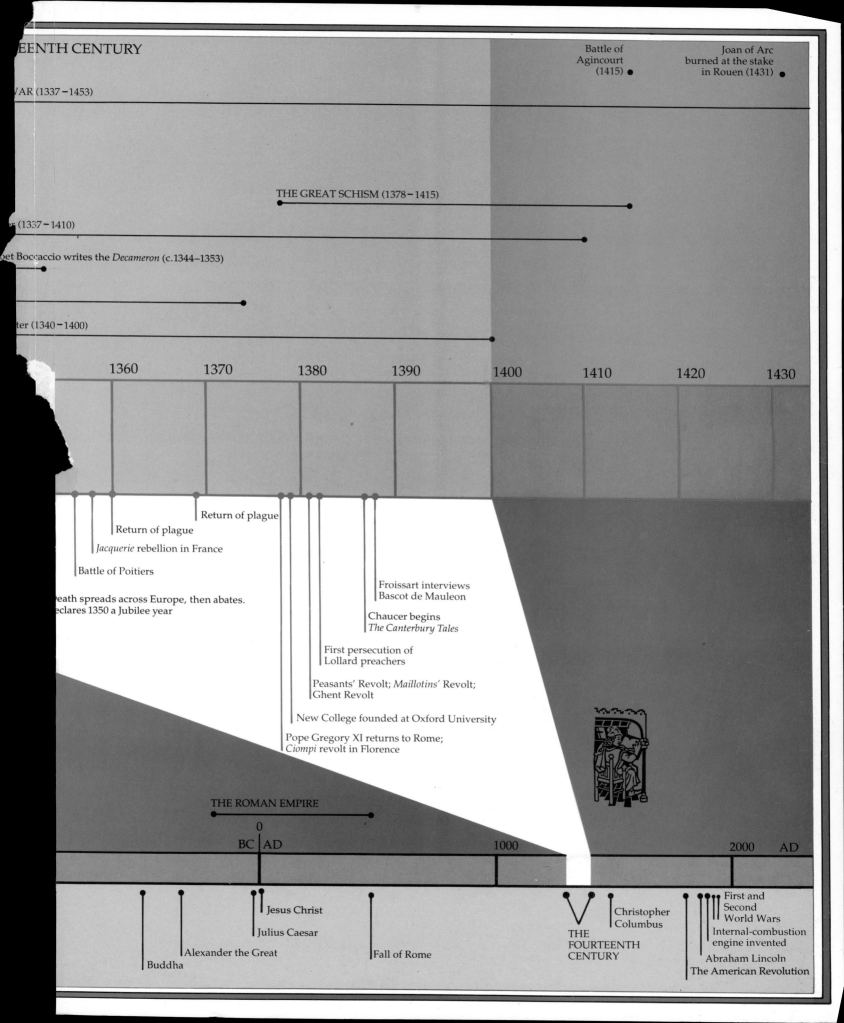

Battle of
Agincourt
(1415) ●

Joan of Arc
burned at the stake
in Rouen (1431) ●

AR (1337–1453)

THE GREAT SCHISM (1378–1415)

(1337–1410)

et Boccaccio writes the *Decameron* (c.1344–1353)

er (1340–1400)

| 1360 | 1370 | 1380 | 1390 | 1400 | 1410 | 1420 | 1430 |

Return of plague

Return of plague

Jacquerie rebellion in France

Battle of Poitiers

eath spreads across Europe, then abates.
eclares 1350 a Jubilee year

Froissart interviews
Bascot de Mauleon

Chaucer begins
The Canterbury Tales

First persecution of
Lollard preachers

Peasants' Revolt; *Maillotins'* Revolt;
Ghent Revolt

New College founded at Oxford University

Pope Gregory XI returns to Rome;
Ciompi revolt in Florence

THE ROMAN EMPIRE

0
BC AD

1000

2000   AD

Jesus Christ

Julius Caesar

Alexander the Great

Buddha

Fall of Rome

THE
FOURTEENTH
CENTURY

Christopher
Columbus

First and
Second
World Wars

Internal-combustion
engine invented

Abraham Lincoln
The American Revolution